faithgirlz

BEST HAIR BOOK EVER!

CUTE CUTS, SWEET STYLES AND TONS OF TRESS TIPS

Produced by Kelsey Haywood

ZONDERKIDZ

Best Hair Book Ever!
Copyright © 2015 Red Engine, LLC

Published in Grand Rapids, Michigan, by Zonderkidz. Zonderkidz is a
registered trademark of The Zondervan Corporation, L.L.C., a wholly
owned subsidiary of HarperCollins Christian Publishing, Inc.

Requests for information should be addressed to
customercare@harpercollins.com.

ISBN 978-0-310-74622-5

Done in association with Red Engine, LLC, Baltimore, MD.

Author: Kelsey Haywood
Editors: Jacque Alberta and Karen Bokram
Contributor: Katie Abbondanza
Cover and interior design: Chun Kim

Printed in Canada

24 25 26 MAR 4 3 2

table of contents

table of contents

Confession: The editors of this book weren't always hairstyling pros. We weren't born knowing how to braid. We certainly struggled through a not-so-nice haircut or two. And we wore a lot of styles that were just fine, but not fabulous. Bored yet?

We sure were. So we decided to trade in our perma-ponytail for a cute, halfsy updo. We put down the flatiron and picked up a bottle of salt spray—and found that underneath all those heat-straightened strands, we had awesome natural waves. We mastered a basic braid, then tried our hand at trickier twists.

Moral of the story? Getting pretty hair is secretly super easy. With a little time and practice (and this book!), you too can have gorgeous strands that give you instant confidence. Just like anything you love, treat your hair with kindness and care. Embrace its uniqueness. And most importantly, have fun with it.

Wishing you infinite good hair days!

—the editors

YOUR BEST HAIR

Hair is like a fingerprint—no one else's is quite like yours. And while it has plenty of aspects that make you feel amazing (vibrant color! bouncy curls!), there might be a few things you're not so crazy about, too (like, sigh, frizz). But here's a secret: Every girl can have terrific tresses. It's all about embracing the mane you were born with, then treating it with TLC. Ready to love your locks? Read on!

A good hair day...every day? Totally doable. In the first part of this book, you'll learn exactly what kind of hair you have—and how to make that mane amazing. We'll help you identify your type and texture (and what those things mean for your hair care regimen). Plus, need a cute cut that flatters your face? Want to grow tresses long and strong? Seeking the secrets to controlling your curls? All those answers (and more!) are in the pages ahead.

NAME YOUR MANE

The first step to enhancing all the amazingness in your strands? Identifying your hair type and texture—and how they affect your hair care routine.

My hair type:

_____

My hair texture:

_____

HAIR TYPE

There are four major hair types: straight, wavy, curly and kinky. To figure out your type, just wash your hair, then gently comb through and allow it to air-dry. Now, check out the four types below and pick which one best describes your strands.

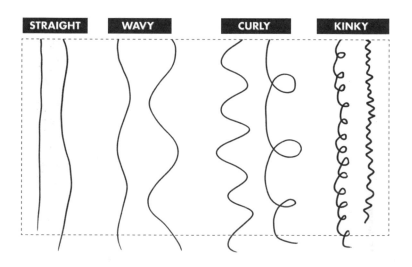

STRAIGHT | WAVY | CURLY | KINKY

STRAIGHT Your strands are sleek and shiny with no bend or wave to them. The good news? Your hair is resistant to damage (congrats!). But getting your styles to hold can be tricky and you tend to get greasy easily.

WAVY These soft, loose waves don't quite form rings—so you can easily rock them straight or curly. The versatility is fab, so switch it up. Just keep an eye out for frizz, a frequent problem.

CURLY Whether your locks straighten out or form ringlets when wet, they'll always dry into a tightly formed "s" pattern. Hide out from humidity, which wreaks major havoc; but super softness and plenty of body make for ultra pretty styling options.

KINKY Your mane is a mix of kinks, twists and coils but strands don't form an "s" pattern and won't change shape when wet or dry. Your major volume is gorgeous, but remember: Since strands tend to be fragile and dry, tons of TLC is always a must.

HAIR TEXTURE

When we talk about texture, we're referring to two things: diameter and density. The diameter of each individual strand of hair indicates whether it's fine, medium or coarse—see below for a breakdown of how to identify your diameter.

Next up is density, which refers to the number of hair follicles on your head—and leads to the classification of either thick (lots of follicles = high density) or thin (fewer follicles = low density). Translation? Your texture will be a combo, like thick/fine or thin/medium. Jot down your personal hairprint, then keep it in mind when caring for your coif.

FINE When rolled between two fingers, a single strand of fine hair is almost impossible to feel.

MEDIUM When rolled between two fingers, a single strand of medium hair will feel like a cotton thread—you know it's there, but it's not rough or super stiff.

COARSE When rolled between two fingers, a single strand of coarse hair feels hard and wiry—you may even hear it crunch.

ROCK YOUR REGIMEN

Just like your body's health depends on basics like brushing your teeth and getting plenty of exercise, your hair requires certain habits to shine. Silky strands start in the shower—so use each time you hop in as an opportunity to treat your tresses to a mini spa session. Follow the basics below, then check out p. 14 to score specialized steps that'll guarantee great locks.

BEGIN WITH A BRUSH. Before you even step into the shower, run a soft-bristled brush through your hair to smooth out those strands and nix any knots—it'll make it way easier to get a thorough wash.

TRY THE RIGHT TEMP. A super steamy shower feels amazing, but too much heat can zap the moisture from your mane and skin. Instead, keep water in the warm range.

MANE MYTH

"THERE'S HAIR IN MY SHOWER DRAIN—IS IT FALLING OUT?!"

Yes—but finding stray hairs in the shower, on your pillow and pretty much everywhere isn't an automatic cause for alarm. It's totally normal for the average female to shed between 50 and 100 hairs per day. Any more, and you should see a doc to check for other issues.

LATHER YOUR LOCKS. Start with a quarter-size amount of shampoo, then apply to soaking wet strands. Massage your entire head with your fingertips—aim for at least 60 seconds to get a good scrub and stimulate your scalp. Make sure to hit the areas above your ears and at the nape of your neck, which are trouble spots for oil and sweat. Add a bit more water and repeat if you feel an extra cleanse is in order. Rinse well.

HIT THE CONDITIONER. Start with a dime-sized amount and apply to the middle section and ends of your hair—skip the scalp. Work it through with your fingers, then rinse well. BTW: The belief that leaving conditioner on longer will make it more effective? A total myth, so no need to waste the extra time.

RINSE AND REPEAT. It's crucial to treat hair to an extremely thorough rinse (sneaky suds that stay will weigh down your locks and cause them to look greasy). Use the coldest water you can handle, which seals the cuticle—a sure way to add shine.

GET A FLY DRY. Before you step out of the shower, gently squeeze the length of your tresses—but don't twist. Hop out, then repeat the squeezing with a towel or t-shirt (see the Tress Trick at right for details). Never, ever rub—or risk breakage. Spritz on a weightless leave-in conditioner spray, then grab a wide-tooth comb and work your way up, beginning with the ends and moving toward the roots. Gently comb through any knots until you've smoothed everything out. Now you're all set to start styling.

ADD SPECIAL STEPS. Flip to p. 14 to find completely customized, health-enhancing tress tips and additions to your regimen.

HAIR DARE # 1

SNAG A SATIN PILLOWCASE

Hello, smooth strands. Snoozing on a cotton case causes kinks and creases, so catch zzz's atop something silky to wake up pretty.

CARE FOR YOUR CURLS

Straight-haired sweeties can skip this section...but if you've been blessed with natural curls (love those cute, bouncy spirals!), then be prepared to show strands some extra attention—or face the wrath of frizz. Just follow these care commandments.

GET SMOOTH. Brush out dry hair before washing, then detangle again in the shower using a wide-tooth comb (while the conditioner is still in). When you're out of the shower, skip the comb and use a tee to dry strands as you gently scrunch.

MIX YOUR FIX. To get crunch-free curls, make a combo cream of serum and mousse. Mix it in your hands, then distribute evenly from roots to tips. Shake head upside down to unlock your curl pattern.

AIR IT OUT… Air-drying is always preferred when possible. Twist curls around your finger to set them in place, then keep hands off and let nature do its thing.

… OR DRY ON THE FLY. In a rush? Pop a cone-shaped diffuser attachment onto your blow dryer, then work in sections to blast warm air on your hair as you gently use fingers to scrunch curls as they dry.

PICK THE PERF PRODUCT. Beach spray will add texture, or try a light pomade mixed with serum for a smooth, bouncy style.

TRY A TEE!

Snag an old T-shirt and cut it along one seam to create an absorbent alternative that's more gentle than a towel for drying your hair—meaning less damage and frizz.

CURLY TRESS TIPS

SHOWER SMARTLY. If your hair is super dry (i.e., crunchy), shampoo just once a week and use a cleansing conditioner rinse on other days.

HANDS OFF. Don't touch your mane after applying product or positioning your curls…or you'll face frizz.

DEFEND YOURSELF. Use a thermal spray before styling to prevent your heat tools from causing any problems.

MAINTAIN MOISTURE. Since curly hair is naturally more dry, using any alcohol-based styling product will only zap more moisture. Skip them.

YOUR GUIDE TO

CHECK ALL THAT ARE TRUE OF Y-O-U...

THEN TRY THESE TRICKS!

- ❑ You're a curly girl.. A, F, J
- ❑ Your hair is straight or wavy .... F
- ❑ You're a blonde (natural) .... D
- ❑ You're a blonde (color-treated) or have highlights .... D, E, J
- ❑ You're a brunette or redhead (natural or not) .... F, H
- ❑ You're constantly in chlorine (hi, swimmers!) .... C, F
- ❑ You've been beaching it up and soaking in saltwater ...... C, F, J
- ❑ You've been using a TON of styling products lately C
- ❑ You treat hair to lots of heat .... G, J
- ❑ You have split ends .... E, G, J
- ❑ You're often oily .... I, J
- ❑ Your hair is dull .... C, F
- ❑ Your hair is flat, fine or limp .... B

HERE'S WHAT TO DO...

A. CO-WASHING
Wash hair with a cleansing cream only—instead of your normal duo—which removes oils from hair's surface while keeping natural sebum within the strand. Skip a day (at least) between washes. FYI: Short for "conditioner washing."

B. VOLUMIZING SHAMPOO
There are tons of options in the drugstore aisle—find one you love and use regularly to lift limp locks.

C. CLARIFYING SHAMPOO
This intense formula will strip hair of residue and build-up—

GORGEOUS HAIR

great for getting a clean canvas, but too drying to use regularly. Only use once a month for a deep cleanse.

D. PURPLE TONING SHAMPOO
Banish brassiness and enhance your hue with this for-blondes-only shampoo. Use it every few washes or just as needed.

E. PROTEIN MASK
These restorative masks employ proteins to rebuild damaged hair. Apply to damp locks, leave on for 15 minutes, then rinse well and let air-dry. Use once or twice weekly as needed.

F. MOISTURIZING MASK
A weekly conditioning treatment is a must for most manes. Apply to damp hair from mid-shaft to ends, leave on for 15 minutes, then rinse well and let air-dry.

G. RETREAT FROM THE HEAT
Stop frying strands and try one of our techniques for waking up with awesome locks—no heat required. Find five fab ideas on p. 42, then use a few each week.

H. HUE-ENHANCING SHAMPOO
Seek specialized suds that bring out the brilliance of your color.

You'll find custom options for most hair colors at the drugstore.

I. SKIP THE SILICONE
Avoid silicone styling products, which can coat the hair and prevent thorough cleansing.

J. KEEP HANDS OFF
Touching and twirling hair causes breakage, frizz and extra oil production. Eek.

THE CUTEST CUT

Long, luxe layers with just a bit of bend…
a textured, razored crop with that rock-
star vibe…a blunt, angled lob that feels
effortlessly chic: Your perfect haircut is
out there, and you'll learn how to find
it right here. How to know when you've
found your style soulmate? It's simple—
you'll beam when you see yourself post
snipping. Oh, and remember: Hair *does*
grow back…so be bold and have fun!

OVAL

ROUND

FIGURE OUT YOUR FACE SHAPE

Have you ever seen a friend right after her totally new haircut and thought, "Wow, she really looks amazing"? The secret to her mini makeover was likely a cut that flattered her face shape.

When it comes to cute cuts, it's all about optics—meaning some styles simply won't look the same on every girl who tries them because everyone has different facial features.

Not sure about your shape? Try this trick: Pull hair into a pony with all strands slicked back, then stand close to a mirror and carefully trace the outline of your face (use a lipstick or a dry-erase marker). Step back, then evaluate what shape you see—oval, round, heart, square...or a unique combination!

CHOOSE THE RIGHT CHOP

Now that you've defined your face shape, score a fiercely flattering snip.

OVAL

YOUR LOOK: Your face is a little longer than it is wide.
YOUR LOCKS: Long layers and blunt styles are fab on you. Oval faces are versatile, so play around with bangs and different parts.

TRY THIS
- Brow-grazing bangs draw major attention to eyes.
- A just-off center part feels fabulously fresh.
- Loose waves add plenty of soft, pretty texture.

ROUND

YOUR LOOK: The width and length of your face are about even, or you have full cheeks and a round chin.

HEART

SQUARE

YOUR LOCKS: Length and layers are your new BFFs. Try an uneven cut (so fun and edgy!) or a mix of layers that start at the jawline.

TRY THIS

- Long, soft layers balance out fullness.
- An awesome, angled cut plays up your adorable, apple-like cheeks.
- Fresh side bangs add interest to the look.

HEART

YOUR LOOK: You have prominent cheekbones or a wider forehead, and your narrow jaw tapers to a point at the chin.

YOUR LOCKS: Try a lob (that's a long bob) that hits just below the jaw. Ask your stylist to keep more length in the front—it'll help highlight your cheekbones.

TRY THIS

- A longer front adds length to your look.
- Some sleekness up top keeps it chic.
- A collarbone length frames your face.

SQUARE

YOUR LOOK: Your forehead is a bit broad and very straight, while your jaw is angular. They're nearly the same width.

YOUR LOCKS: Go for angled strands in the front to soften a defined jaw. Half-up hair is so pretty on you.

TRY THIS

- Long bangs mean you can play around with your part.
- Below-the-ear waves soften your jaw.
- Some piecey-ness in the front keeps the look extra feminine.

GET A CUTE CROP

So you've identified your hair type, hair texture and face shape. Yay! But before you go anywhere near a stylist's chair for that big chop, you've got a bit more hair homework.

SNAG SOME STYLE INSPIRATION

Flip through magazines and scour the internet to find images of locks you love. Even if a cut isn't great for your face shape, a skilled stylist can often incorporate elements of what you like.

DISCUSS THE CUT

At the start of your appointment, ask for a full consultation to chat about the perfect chop (and keep in mind that some stylists will want you to set this up prior to the day of your cut, so make sure to ask when you schedule). First, show your pro all your hair inspiration—and be super specific about why it's in your stack (like a certain length, color, layers or shape). Then tell her about any hair habits that'll affect your upkeep. You only want to come back for cuts twice a year? You prefer to spend less than five minutes styling your strands in the morning? You pull hair into a pony every single day? These factors matter when creating a cut that'll fit into your lifestyle, so be honest about what you're willing to do for fab hair.

TAKE NOTES ON TECHNIQUE

Ask your stylist to finish your snip session with a pro blowout. As your hair gets flipped and dried to perfection, take notes on her moves and ask plenty of questions so you can replicate the technique at home. More blowout tips on p. 24.

MANE MYTH

DOES CUTTING YOUR HAIR MAKE IT GROW?

Chopping ends often certainly won't make hair sprout from your scalp any quicker or increase the number of hair follicles on your head (sorry!). But now for the good news: Frequent trims will nix damaged ends, which creates the illusion of fullness and also keeps split ends from creeping up the hair shaft. Ask a pro stylist to recommend how long you should go between cuts (it varies based on your hair health).

HAIR
DARE #2

BE BOLD

A faux hawk? A pink pixie? Nope, extreme styles aren't for everyone—but you know what is? The mega confidence it takes to rock them. Just do what you love, and you'll love how you look.

PICK THE PERFECT SET OF STYLING PRODUCTS

On a trip to any drugstore, you'll find hundreds of bottles and tubes in the hair care aisle. These prettifying potions are ultra important when styling your mane, so experiment with different formulas and ask around for recommendations.

Any time you're working with product, it's best to use the smallest dab possible and add more later. A general rule of thumb is to use a quarter-size amount of mousses and creams, while serums and oils should only be dime-sized. When it comes to sprays, start with a light mist. Also key? The placement of your product. If you're after volume, start scrunching at the root and work your way to the ends. Aiming for more moisture or repair? Start at your ends, where hair is more likely to be damaged.

STYLING SHOPPING LIST

- ☐ BEACH OR SALT SPRAY: Create texture and waves in wet hair
- ☐ DRY SHAMPOO: Mask oily hair and refresh
- ☐ HAIRSPRAY: Finish and hold
- ☐ HEAT OR THERMAL PROTECTOR: Minimize damage
- ☐ LEAVE-IN CONDITIONER SPRAY: Soften and detangle
- ☐ MOUSSE: Volume and hold
- ☐ OIL (LIKE ARGAN) OR SERUM: Add shine, smooth and defrizz
- ☐ POMADE: Texture and separation
- ☐ STYLING OR SCULPTING CREAM: Light hold and support
- ☐ TEXTURIZING SPRAY: Create texture in dry hair

GROW TO GREAT LENGTHS

Longing for longer locks? Whether you're growing out a pixie or working your way to Rapunzel status, follow these mane mantras.

HEAD FIRST

To go long, start at the top—and that means your scalp. At least two times a week in the shower, give your scalp a 60-second massage using a shampoo with peppermint or eucalyptus (these essential oils increase scalp circulation and promote growth). Then follow up with a deep conditioning mask.

SKIP THE SHAMPOO

Keep in mind that washing hair can also strip it of natural oils—which can dry it out and lead to breakage. Shampoo only every other day, then experiment with ways to wash less frequently. One idea? After a shampoo and blow-dry one day, skip washing the next day and curl your locks instead. On the third day, try a trendy topknot. Dry shampoo fixes any slickness.

tress trick

HOLD THE HEAT

High temps snap strands, so the less you use your heat tools, the faster your hair will grow. Let your hair air-dry 75 percent before blow-drying. Or add a smoothing serum to your damp 'do and sleep on it before a speedy straightening session in the morning. And when you do hit the heat? Use a thermal protecting spray.

FIND A MANE MUSE

Thanks to their full-time glam squads, celebs always seem to have awesome hair and endless styles. Reap the benefits by seeking a star with a similar cut and texture to your own as inspiration. She'll never know!

GET YOUR VITAMINS

Just like the rest of your bod, hair health is dependent on a balanced diet filled with vitamins and nutrients. Take a daily multivitamin (ask your doctor to make a recommendation), then fill up your plate with superfoods like salmon, walnuts, eggs, carrots, spinach and blueberries. Sounds like a yummy salad!

STRESS LESS
If you're anxious, your hair will take a hit. Relax with a run, yoga or a pedi and froyo date with your bestie—then sit back and chill your way to sleek strands.

FAKE IT WITH FRINGE
This quick tip makes locks look longer: Ask your stylist to cut blunt bangs, which instantly create the illusion of length.

MAKE THE CUT
Speaking of snipping: When your goal is to grow, how often should you really get a cut? Aim for every five or six months, and only take off a quarter-inch at a time. Your goal is just to trim any split ends before they start sneaking up the hair shaft.

+ TRESS S.O.S.

" *I butchered my bangs!* "

Maybe you were obsessed with the piecey bang look—until you tried it. Or maybe you got a bit too snippy with the scissors when trimming your bangs at home. But no matter what happened, these remedies rock for growing out bad bangs...

BRAIDS Sweep hair into a deep side part and try two face-framing French braids on each side. If any short pieces pop out, it'll just add to a messy-chic look.

BOBBIES Twist bangs straight back or to the side, then pop in a pin to hold them in place. See p. 93 for creative ways to rock them.

HEADBANDS Sporty and stretchy, glitzy and glam—there are plenty of bands to stylishly sweep bangs back.

HATS A funky fedora, cozy knit beanie and sporty cap are just a few of the stylish headwear options that'll hide any horror on your head.

HOW TO SNAG SALON STYLE... EVERY DAY!

1. Pull aside bangs, then secure the rest of hair in a low, loose bun. Dry this section first — the front is most important!

2. Unclip hair and work in a drop of serum. Use fingers to tousle hair while applying heat until 75 percent dry.

3. Grab the section at the nape of your neck, then pull the rest up. Fully dry this section until smooth.

4. Section off the two top layers on both sides of your part, then dry the bottom sections all around.

5. Drop a top section out of a clip and fully dry. Lift and focus at the root to add pretty volume. Repeat on the other side.

6. Seal, shine and set your blowout: Turn your dryer onto the cool setting and run through each section one more time.

PRO BLOWOUT

BLOWOUT BASICS

START WITH A SQUEEZE
Never start with soaking wet strands—your products won't distribute well and more blow-drying means more heat damage). Gently squeeze small sections all over.

NIX THE KNOTS
Use a wide-tooth comb or paddle brush to detangle damp strands. The trick: Start at the ends of your hair, then slowly work your way up until everything is smooth.

ROCK THE ROOTS
If your roots are dried well, everything else will fall prettily into place. Grab a section of hair near the scalp with your brush, then gently pull straight up as you apply heat.

TAKE AIM
Think of your hair like shingles on a roof—each strand has a ton of teeny layers that should stay flat and smooth. Always aim air down the shaft, toward your ends.

MAKE IT LAST
Extend your blowout by pulling hair into a loose bun at night and securing with a scrunchy (no creases!). In the a.m., spritz on dry shampoo.

SECTIONING SECRETS

Here's the map to your mane...

1 Grab your bangs and front pieces

2 + 3 Draw a line from ear to ear, then split down the middle

4 Pull nape area aside

5 Everything else!

SCHOOL HAIR

Introducing the new class of A+ looks: twists, braids and ponies that are sure to land you on the yearbook's best-tressed list. Pulled-back 'dos keep hair from falling in your face (crucial when you're concentrating on a quiz) while quick-and-easy embellishments add just enough polish (perfect when you're campaigning for class prez). Study up on these smart styles.

reverse French topknot

32

y twist

peppy pony

38

36

30

braid bar

34

the sweet sidewinder

reverse French **topknot**

This braid is best when you're familiar with French braiding (see p. 118 for our handy how-to). Remember, practice makes perfect — and braiding upside down gets easier every time. Promise.

MORE FUN WITH BUNS...

Make it majorly messy. So sweet!

Wrap a headband or necklace around your knot. Easy.

Pigtail buns are so pretty—and princess-approved.

1. Flip your head upside down so strands hang toward the floor, then brush everything straight down to make all your hair completely smooth.

2. Rub a dollop of mousse between your hands, then work it through hair from roots to tips.

3. Grab the section of hair at the nape of your neck, then separate it into three equal parts.

4. Cross the left section over the middle section, then the right section over the middle section.

5. Pick up more hair to join the left and right sections, then repeat to continue French braiding.

6. Once you've reached the crown of your head, tie off the braid with a mini elastic.

7. While you're still upside down, gather the end of the braid and all other hair into a pony and tie off with a strong elastic.

8. Braid the entire pony regularly, then use a clear elastic to tie off the ends.

9. Wrap your braid around the base of the pony, then secure with pins and finish with hairspray.

Here's something to cheer for — a pony that's fab, flattering and fast to throw together. Score!

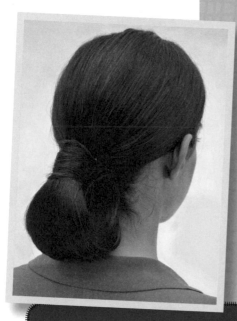

1. Give hair a gentle, all-over tease (get the how-to on p.111.

2. Grab all the hair from the top of your head to about eye level, from your hairline to the crown, and give that section a bit more backcombing to create plenty of body up top.

3. Use your fingers or a wide-tooth comb to brush all hair back off your face, and secure in a pony right below the crown.

4. Using a long tail comb, push it through the top of hair and gently lift—you're creating that pretty poof effect up top.

5. Grab a 1½" or 2" curling iron, then flip the ends up.

6. Take a small section of hair from underneath the pony, then wrap it around the tie. Secure with a bobby pin and mist all over with hair spray.

Try This

Take your tail from peppy to polished with this smooth styling trick: Simply flip the ends under—and pin—to create a luxe loop. This works best on a low pony, so make sure to start near the nape of your neck.

peppy **pony**

the sweet sidewinder

This playful 'do is a cinchy way for naturalistas and cropped-cut cuties to freshen up their shorter styles. Tight twists create a faux-hawk effect—and keep all the emphasis on your smiling face.

1 Use a tail comb to divide your hair into three sections: left side, right side and middle. Clip everything in the middle together (and out of the way) so you can work on the sides.

2 Starting above one ear, twist straight back along the side of your head. Keep everything tight by gathering and tucking more hair as you go.

3 When you reach the ends of your hair (or the back of your head), slide in a few bobby pins. Repeat on the other side.

4 Unclip middle section and use a comb to rake all hair closely to the side of either part. Pop in pins along the bottom to keep the fauxhawk in place, and use gel if you need extra hold.

✳ GET PERFECT HAIR FOR PICTURE DAY ✳

Want a school photo you'll actually love? Here's how to prep...

- Grab a handful of flattering photos of yourself, then take note: How are you wearing your hair? Pick a style you love that looks great on camera.

- Remember: Don't hide behind your hair—keep it off your face for the prettiest snap. Try pulling long tresses over one shoulder or rocking a half-up 'do.

- Practice your look a week before photo day. Style your strands in the morning, then make sure those locks can last until it's time to say cheese.

- Bring a mini mirror, brush, hairspray and dry shampoo for tiny touchups before the big moment. Go easy on the dry shampoo, though—it can dull locks. Follow up with a bit of hairspray to create some shine.

- Sit up straight and smile!

Even knotting newbies can master this twisting trick. Here, two basic braids get crossed atop a bun—but the look also functions flawlessly with a half-up/half-down style, too.

" Umm...is that GUM?! "

First up, don't freak out—no need to grab the scissors! Calmly walk to the closest mirror, then pull all of your unstuck hair out of the way and tie it back. Now you've got two options to get out the gum: the classic ice remedy (apply ice to the trouble spot for at least 15 minutes, or until it has hardened enough to remove the hair), or oil. And by "oil," we actually mean any of the following: peanut butter, silicone hair serum or cooking oil. Apply generously all over the gum and the stuck hair, then wait a few minutes while the oils break down the gum. Gently comb out, then wash your locks.

1. Prep and part hair however you'd like (try brushing it straight back, like our model, or sweep strands into a side part for a halfsie style).

2. Grab the longest possible section of hair from the area above both ears. The more hair you use, the thicker your braid bar will be.

3. Braid both sections of hair and tie off with clear elastics. Once secure, gently tug on the braid to make it thicker and flatter.

4. If you're wearing hair down, skip to the next step. If you're wearing it in a bun, pull all non-braided pieces back into a pony and secure above the nape of your neck. Wrap the tail around the base, then secure with pins.

5. Pull both braided pieces back and across the other. Tuck the ends underneath and pin. Mist all over with hairspray.

braid bar

y twist

For all those times you've got 30 seconds to style before running out the door, meet your new bestie: the Y Twist. Quick and easy, this pony prettifier is your go-to remedy for rushed mornings.

1. Give strands a quick mist of hairspray, then run a brush from roots to tips.

2. Grab a large section of hair from both sides of head (right above and behind your ears), then pull those forward and pull everything else into a pony. Secure with an elastic.

3. Slip a tie around your wrist, then grab a loose section in each hand and twist both backward. When you reach the pony, combine all three sections and secure with a tie.

4. Grab a section of hair from the bottom of the pony, then wrap around the ties and secure with a bobby pin. Mist with spray, then run out the door!

More things to do with your pony...

- Get a perfect party look with slick-backed strands and a super sleek tail.

- Split into two halves, twist each, then twist them around each other. Rope braid!

- Tease the tail then spritz with texturizer for a chic, messy look.

- Stack two ponytails a few inches apart to create the illusion of a longer, fuller tail. Curl the ends to keep it camouflaged.

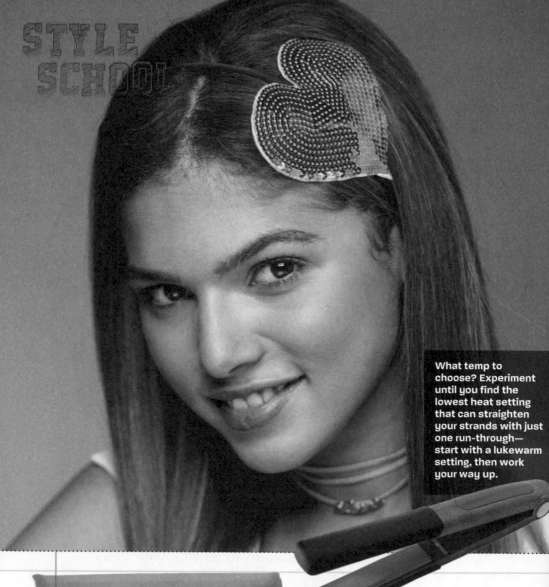

STYLE SCHOOL

What temp to choose? Experiment until you find the lowest heat setting that can straighten your strands with just one run-through—start with a lukewarm setting, then work your way up.

The straight talk

The smoothest and shiniest strands often get their supreme straightness with the help of a flatiron. Want your own perfectly pressed tresses? Here's how...

- Snag a quality flatiron with a dial or multiple heat settings—it's über important that you keep control of the temperature (get more about that in the pink box above).
- Never apply heat to wet or bare hair. Instead, dry your mane completely and then prep locks with a thermal heat protectant spray before you style.

- Section hair horizontally into two layers (or try three if your hair is super thick). Clip away the top layer.
- Starting on one side and working your way around, grab 2" sections and brush through.
- In one smooth motion, gently press the clamps down near the root and run the flatiron down the length of your hair. When you reach the tips, twist your wrist up or under if you want a bit of flip.
- Move on to the next section until you've reached the other side of your head, then let down the top layer and repeat.

HAIR Candy

Statement Bobbies

Make a statement—literally—with pins emblazoned with the words that matter most. Slip one on solo (try your name) or team up a trio (like dream, love, hope).

WHAT YOU'LL NEED

- Alphabet pasta
- Spray paint
- Bobby pins
- Craft glue
- Manila folder or cardstock
- Old newspaper

1 Pop your bobby pins onto the edge of the cardstock or folder, then lay out all your letters in order.

2 Cover the flat side of your first bobby with a thin layer of craft glue, then carefully place the letters (using either your fingers or tweezers, whichever is easier for you).

3 Repeat until you've placed words on all your bobbies, then let dry completely.

4 Grab a parent and head outside. Lay the folder on top of the newspaper, then cover with a light mist of spray paint. Let dry, then add another layer if you want more coverage.

5 Let dry completely, then turn the folder over and repeat on the back side of the pin. Once everything is dry, remove from the cardstock and style!

Great hair...

while you sleep!

Want to add more minutes to your morning? Save styling time by snoozing your way to great strands. Just prep before bed...then wake up with dream hair.

FOR BEACHY WAVES...
Spritz damp hair with salt spray and twist into two French pigtails (get the how-to on p. 118). Let dry overnight, then release in the morning and spritz with texturizing spray for definition.

FOR TOUSLED TEXTURE...
Separate dry strands into six sections—three on each side of your head. Starting a few inches away from the root, braid each section and loosely tie off, leaving an inch of ends hanging out. Apply a mist of leave-in conditioning spray, then let dry. In the a.m., blast with dry shampoo and tousle.

FOR KEEPING CURLS SMOOTH...
Girls with natural or super kinky hair can keep curls from getting smashed during sleep by pineappling: the fun (and fruity) term for gathering all your hair on the top of your head, then loosely wrapping a scarf around it. The secret? Make sure it's silk, as other fabrics will suck out moisture and cause frizz.

FOR BODY IN SHORT STRANDS...
Get proactive with your dry shampoo and apply generously to roots before you hit the sheets—it'll soak up any oil that develops overnight, and you'll wake up with perfect muss-and-go texture.

FOR A BIT OF BEND...
Apply a lightweight sculpting cream to slightly damp strands, then twist hair into two topknots, pigtail-style, on the top of your head. Secure with jumbo hairpins and release in a.m. for subtle wave.

CHAPTER

4

SUMMER HAIR

The sunny season has a signature style all its own: laid-back and effortless, of course, but always amped up with fun accents and a dash of beach-babe boldness. The how-tos ahead add interest to classic looks (think: dressing up a Dutch braid with neon ribbons) and maximize your natural texture to keep styling simple (like a hippie-inspired head-band that's best on bedhead). It's your time to shine—so get out there and glow.

48

woven ribbon

bohemian band

50

52

kiss of color

56

regal roll

54

mega braid

woven **ribbon**

This 30-second styling trick is a brilliant way to summer-ize your braids.

1 Find the point where you'll start your braid, then measure from that point to the ends of your hair.

2 Cut three ribbons to that length, then tie all together in a single knot at one end. Set aside.

3 Start braiding above one ear—a Dutch looks lovely (check out the how-to on p.120), but feel free to switch it up. If your hair is long enough, bring the braid around the hairline at your neck and finish over the opposite shoulder. Secure with an elastic.

4 Grab your ribbons and tuck the knotted top underneath the start of your braid. Secure with a bobby pin.

5 Randomly wrap, pin and twist the ribbons down the length of your braid. Some can be pulled underneath sections of hair and truly twisted around, while others can simply be placed on top and pinned. Don't think about it too much—no need to make it perfect.

6 When you get to the end, wrap excess ribbon around the elastic and tie off. Mist everything with hairspray to set.

Try This

Make a subtler statement by working ribbon into a 2" bitty braid. Pull over your shoulder, then curl the rest.

Dipped tips are a trendy touch on summer strands — and a pretty way to play with temporary color.

"Ouch...I burned my scalp!"

Not good! Next time, prevent this problem by always wearing a hat when out in the sun. And if you must expose those strands? Mist your entire scalp with an SPF spray for hair (find one at drugstores), then pull hair straight back into a pony (no part = less chance of burning). How to fix your current situation? Flakes are unavoidable as your damaged skin starts to heal—but you can soothe your scalp with a rinse of apple cider vinegar (just mix equal parts cider and water, then pour onto freshly washed strands and let dry).

1. Snag some hair chalk (you can find it at most salons, drugstores and plenty of online retailers).

2. Style hair any way you want: Try a fab faux-hawk, pumped-up pony or loose waves. Just make sure your hair is dry!

3. Apply hair chalk to your ends only—aim for about an inch. If your hair is straight, be consistent all over. If your hair is curly (like the model at right), just grab a few random pieces all over.

4. To set the color, mist with hairspray. Wash your hands to remove any excess chalk.

Most hair chalk will wash out with one or two shampoos. If you're dealing with stubborn color—and need it gone, fast—wash with a cleansing shampoo, specially formulated to safely strip your strands.

kiss of color

bohemian band

Get set for festival season with this throwback fave: a haute, hippie-inspired 'do that pairs perfectly with a messy mane.

1 Start with wavy, texturized strands. Mist with a bit of dry shampoo (it'll help your headband stay put later).

2 Sweep hair into a side part, then gently tease the roots of both sides.

3 Slip an elastic headband straight down around your head—the band should be level with the top of your forehead.

4 Grab the sides of the band and gently push upward to create extra body up top. Finish with a bit of hairspray to hold.

Try This

Cute on cropped cuts, too! The key: Pair plenty of volume up top with textured ends.

Hey, flower child! Get this fresh look by snagging a floral crown— find pretty picks on Etsy.

Twist tons of texture into your tresses for a braid of braids—pretty to look at, and cinchy to style.

MANE MYTH

DOES LEMON JUICE REALLY GIVE YOU HIGHLIGHTS?

It can—but that doesn't mean you should try it. Although some natural hair remedies recommend lemon juice as an alternative to chemical highlighting treatments, it's also extremely acidic and unpredictable. Translation: While a bit of lemon juice and water might turn your fair-haired bestie into a beautiful blonde, it can also streak strands to look orange and brassy—or worse, leave it damaged. Better to leave lightening to a pro.

HAIR
DARE #3

FIX A FLAW

Saddened by split ends? Fed up with frizz? Pick your #1 hair nightmare and research a remedy. *(FYI: Regular trims and deep conditioning treatments fix those tricky situations, if you're wondering.)*

1 Split hair into three equal sections: left, middle and right.

2 Pull left and right sections aside and clip out of the way.

3 Split the middle section into two unequal sections: one large and one small. Braid both sections, creating a big braid and a little braid. Secure each braid with mini elastics.

4 Take a tiny portion of hair from the right section and twist it into a bitty braid. Secure braid with an elastic.

5 Loosely braid all three sections of hair together. Secure with an elastic and cover with a mini ribbon.

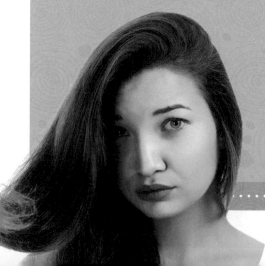

mega braid

regal roll

This sophisticated style is a lifesaver when strands need to switch from playful to polished. Perfect on wet hair, too — pool-party approved!

1. Split hair into an extreme side part, then brush hair smooth on both sides.

2. On the heavier side, grab a large section of hair at the top of your part and start rolling it inward and down your hairline, bringing in more hair as you go and pulling it tightly.

3. Continue working around the head. When you reach the nape of your neck, sweep back the hair from the other side and twist it all into a bun. Secure with an elastic and a bit of spray.

Try This

Double up! Sweeties with shorter strands can roll from both sides and pin together in the back.

STYLE SCHOOL

Behold the conical curling wand, your new bestie for making major waves.

Beach waves 101!

Take summer hair straight into the school year—and beyond—with this how-to for creating tousled twists.

- Spritz dry hair with a dry texturizing spray and gently brush to distribute throughout all of your strands.
- Separate hair into three sections (left, right and front) by parting down the center and pulling bangs aside.
- Hold the curling wand upside down and wrap a 1" section of hair around the barrel, leaving out the bottom inch.
- Repeat on all sections, switching the direction you wrap (first toward the face, then away) for mega texture.
- Mist hair lightly with hairspray, then let it completely cool for 15 minutes—the perfect time to finish getting ready.
- Loosen curls by running a wide-tooth comb through them (be gentle!), then finish with a bit of spray for shine.

HAIR Candy

Boho Braid Wrap

This bohemian embellishment adds festival-approved flare to any style. Twist around the length of a side pony, or tie off a basic braid and let the ends hang loose.

WHAT YOU'LL NEED

- Leather cord
- Suede cord
- Beads
- Craft feathers
- Craft glue

WHAT YOU'LL DO

1 Cut the leather cord and suede cord into two equal lengths—experiment with the size and go shorter if you have a cropped cut or longer if you have more hair to wrap.

2 Combine the two cords by tying together with three knots: one knot in the middle, and then one knot 2 inches away from both ends.

3 Grab the excess leather cord at both ends, then pop on a few beads and tie off to secure.

4 Attach the feathers to the suede cord by dipping the quill in a bit of craft glue, then sliding a bead onto the cord and tucking the quill into the bead. Tie off the bead and let dry.

5 Repeat on the other end. Get creative with bead patterns—you can space them out with knots, or stack a few together.

6 Let dry, then wrap around a pigtail or ponytail for an earthy accent piece.

Summer hair bummers

Scorching temps and plenty of pool time don't have to lead to lame locks. Our tricks fix the trickiest of summer hair sitches.

HAIR BUMMER #1: FIERCE FRIZZ

Hair can go haywire in the humidity, but it's totally possible to land sleekness in the summer. Always wash with a hydrating shampoo and conditioner, then apply a dime-sized dab of smoothing cream to damp hair. Aim to air-dry whenever possible.

HAIR BUMMER #2: DULL DRYNESS

Add a once-a-week deep conditioning treatment to your routine—you can grab plenty of luxe treatments at the drugstore, or try our DIY how-to on p. 94. After you apply, pop on a shower cap and let conditioner soak in for at least 15 minutes. Rinse like crazy, then let your hair air-dry.

HAIR BUMMER #3: BAD BRASSINESS

Blondies have been griping about green tresses since the advent of the in-ground. No matter your color, prevent damage and discoloration by wetting hair in the shower before diving into the pool or ocean. If your strands are already soaked with clean H2O, less chlorine and saltwater can seep in. Brilliant! Don't forget to rinse off post-swim, too, so the salt and chemicals don't cause damage.

HAIR BUMMER #4: GROSS GREASINESS

Between the heat and hormones, slick strands are as common as the ice-cream truck come summertime. Nix the urge to wash and repeat—too much cleansing can cause your scalp to produce more oil. Stretch time between suds with this brilliant technique for applying dry shampoo: Instead of spritzing it all over, spray a light mist down your part, then muss with fingers. Move over an inch and create another part, repeating until you've hit all the trouble spots. Wash every other day, if possible. Greasiness gone!

.busted!

Salt Spray Texturizer

For beautifully beachy strands, a quick mist of this sea salt spray mimics the wave-enhancing wonders of a day at the shore. Here's what you'll need...

- Spray bottle
- 1 cup hot water
- 1 tsp sea salt (or more for a beachier look)
- 1 tbsp coconut oil
- 1 tbsp leave-in conditioner

WHAT YOU'LL DO

1. Measure out ingredients.
2. Add all (except water) to the spray bottle.
3. Pour hot water into the spray bottle, over the ingredients. Secure the nozzle and then shake for 30 to 60 seconds, until everything is dissolved.
4. Spray on damp strands. Scrunch, then allow hair to air-dry and style.

SPORTY HAIR

From hitting the pavement to ruling the court, you're a girl on the go—and you need a team of tress tricks that can keep up with your insane schedule of run club, yoga class, practice sessions and game days. Introducing our all-star styles that'll keep those locks on lock-down—no matter what an opponent (or life!) throws your way. And the total game-changer? They're fierce enough for the field, but so cute you'll want to rock them everywhere.

fierce French

double-Dutch fishtails

68

70

bubble pony

66

72

bitty braids

74

spider pony

fierce French

This twisted topper is the perfect style to sport all day—from school, to your lacrosse game, to a study session later on. First rock the look with your locks down, then pull everything up into a power pony when it's time to play.

1 Start with wavy strands—either curl your hair all over, or simply wake up with a bit of texture using one of our tricks on p. 42.

2 Grab all the hair from the tip top of your head—that's everything in between the ends of both eyebrows, from your hairline to your crown.

3 Grab three small sections of strands from up front, then French braid till you hit the crown (find the how-to on p. 118).

4 Secure with an elastic, then wrap a small section of hair around the base and pop in a pin to keep in place. Let the rest hang in waves.

More sporty style ideas

- Sweep curly strands into a poofy pony, then top with a bold wrap.

- Pair a set of stretchy headbands. Bonus points for body in the middle.

- Work team-colored ribbons into a basic braid.

- Dip tips of a pony in a spirited hue of hair chalk.

- Pull hair into a high pony, tie it off, then braid it. Done!

This easy update amps the intensity of your plain pony. Pretty on pigtails, too!

1 Grab a handful of hair ties in a cute color scheme, then pull hair into a pony at the nape of your neck.

2 Place another tie about two or three inches below the base, then wrap it around till it's tight and gently push upward to create a bubble.

3 Repeat until you've reached the bottom of your pony, and allow at least an inch or two of ends to hang loose.

Try This

The bubble pony can go sophisticated, sweet or sporty—depending on how you style it. For a game, grab ties in your school's colors. For a sleeker look, use mini elastics. For a dance, add accessories!

bubble pony

double-Dutch fishtails

Fierce yet feminine, these edgy hybrid pigtails combine two bold braids for a double dose of game-winning drama.

1. Rub a dollop of mousse through strands, then brush through to distribute evenly.

2. Use a tail comb to part hair down the center and separate into two equal sections.

3. Rub a bit of volumizing powder between your hands, then start Dutch braiding from your top hairline to the nape of your neck on one side.

4. Once you reach the bottom hairline, combine all sections of your Dutch braid and begin again—this time, though, twist into a fishtail.

5. Continue to braid until you reach the very ends of your hair, then tie off with a mini clear elastic.

6. Use your fingers to gently pull on the fishtailed section—it'll make it thicker, looser and add a little more texture.

7. Repeat on the other side.

Want to keep hair out of the way (and off your shoulders)? When you're ready to switch to the fishtail, just merge both pigtails together and braid into a single strand. Find the Dutch how-to on p. 120 and the fishtail tutorial on p. 122.

Whether you're running in a track meet or just rocking your cutest track jacket, a pair of awesome accent braids are your new MVPs.

MAY
25

HAIR
DARE #4

WORK A WEEK
OF NEW 'DOS

Challenge yourself to try a different style every day for a week. It's not always easy—but when you push yourself to keep it creative, you'll discover plenty of pretty new ideas.

1 Sweep hair into a deep side part.

2 On the lighter side of hair, grab a small, 1" section near the part line and begin to Dutch braid or cornrow. Move straight back along the part, then dip down toward your neck.

3 When you get to the same height as your ear, stop braiding against the scalp and braid the rest of the section regularly. Tie off.

4 Grab another section of hair below the first row and repeat.

5 Use a 1½" barrel to curl any loose hair, then mist with texturizing spray all over.

Find our cornrow tutorial on p. 124 and more microbraiding tips on p. 126.

bitty braids

spider pony

When multiple braids team up for a stunning statement pony, you'll be the fiercest player on the field. Try it with four "legs" like our model — or step it up to six.

tress trick

1. Use a comb to part hair neatly into five sections: your bangs and front pieces, then two large sections on each side of your head. Clip everything out of the way.

2. Let down a side section, then Dutch braid (see p. 120) in a straight direction from the hairline to the crown. Flip upside down if necessary. When you reach the crown, tie off remaining hair with a mini elastic.

3. Repeat on that side's other section. Switch to the next side and repeat.

4. Grab your front section, then gently tease at the root before brushing back. Pop in a bobby to keep the poof in place.

5. Combine the ends of all sections in a pony at the crown, then secure with a strong elastic. Take a one-inch section and wrap around the base, then pin.

6. Tease the length of the pony to add a bit of volume and messy texture. Mist everything with spray to set.

PUMP UP YOUR PONY

For a pony that won't budge during your next game or major workout session, simply stack two or three hair ties on top of each other for major support.

HAIR
DARE #5

TACKLE ONE
TRICKY TUTORIAL

Hit up YouTube or Pinterest to find a stunning style you're obsessed with, then practice 'til you hit tress perfection.

Custom Dry Shampoo

WHAT YOU'LL NEED

- 1/4 cup cornstarch
- Lavender or peppermint essential oil
- Empty, clean spice shaker with perforated lid
- Plus...
  IF YOU'RE A BRUNETTE: 2 tbsp unsweetened cocoa powder
  IF YOU'RE A REDHEAD: 2 tbsp cinnamon
  IF YOU'RE A BLONDE: 2 tbsp baking soda

WHAT YOU'LL DO

1 IF YOU'RE A BRUNETTE: Combine a quarter-cup of cornstarch with 2 tablespoons of unsweetened cocoa powder.
   IF YOU'RE A REDHEAD: Combine a quarter-cup of cornstarch with 2 tablespoons of cinnamon.
   IF YOU'RE A BLONDE: Combine a quarter-cup of cornstarch with 2 tablespoons of baking soda.

2 FOR ALL: Pour into a bowl, then add a few drops of essential oil (if desired)—lavender is great for all hair types and has a soothing and calming effect, while energizing peppermint is perfect if oiliness is a problem. Stir, then pour into your container. Close the lid and shake.

3 FOR ALL: To use, sprinkle directly onto strands and muss with your fingers. Or, pour some into your hand and sweep it up with a clean, large blush brush, then swirl onto trouble spots. Brush out any excess and you're good to go!

HAIR Candy

Leather Pony Tie

And that's a wrap! This one-step style is the cinchiest way you can up the pretty factor on a plain pony.

WHAT YOU'LL NEED

- 8" x 1" strip of leather (find at craft supply stores or more options on Etsy)
- Sewing shears
- Ruler
- Pencil

WHAT YOU'LL DO

1. Lay your piece of leather on a flat surface with the good side facing down.

2. Using a ruler and pencil, make one straight line going down the entire length of leather.

3. Measure one inch over, then make another parallel line.

4. At the edges of the leather between the outline, sketch on slanted lines to create triangular tips at both ends.

5. Have a friend or parent hold the leather taught while you carefully cut along your outline—a ruler helps, too, if your hands are shaky.

6. Pull hair into a pony, then wrap the leather once or twice around the base and tie. Easy!

WILL SWEATING IN A PONY BREAK MY HAIR?

Nope! Working out in a pony is totally fine—
as long as you follow these rules…

#1 SPRITZ STRANDS WITH DRY SHAMPOO
FIRST. No, we're not asking you to get all
glam for a sweat sesh—but dry shampoo will
zap sweat on the spot so things don't get out of
control up there.

#2 DON'T PULL THE PONY SUPER TIGHT.
All that pulling and tightness can cause
breakage and, eventually, lead to seriously
damaged strands. Instead, try a low pony (it's
less likely to fall as you move) and slip on a
grippy headband to keep fly-aways at bay.

#3 LET HAIR DOWN RIGHT AFTER YOUR
WORKOUT. Don't let sweat dry while it's
still up (which leads to, you guessed it, more
damage). Instead, release hair and gently run
a soft-bristle brush through it to distribute oils.
Once you've cooled down, apply a bit more dry
shampoo until you can give it a real wash.

WEEKEND HAIR

You rule the weekend. Friday night?
You're hosting your volleyball team's
fundraising fête. Saturday? That's spent
volunteering at the animal shelter before
a glam get-together with the girls. And
Sunday? First church, then off to brunch
with your family. Your hairstyles have to
be easy—nothing crazy and complicated
here, please!—but also pretty and
polished. Enter five fab 'dos that are
a cinch to style…even if you sleep in
occasionally. Shhh, we won't tell.

braid ladder

86

twisted pony

90

fishtail bun

88

84

headband wrap

92

pinned perfection

braid ladder

Stack a few simple braids atop each other for a cinchy style that works on any hair length. Shorties can join braids together with mini knots. Have longer locks? Leave the rest down for a pretty half 'do.

1. Split strands into three sections horizontally: top, middle and bottom. Pull the middle and bottom layers aside and secure.

2. Gently tease the roots of the top section, then brush it all straight back. Divide ends into three sections, then braid for about an inch. Secure with bobby pins.

3. Unclip the middle section and divide into left half and right half. Starting on either side, braid against the side of your head until you reach the middle.

4. Repeat on the other side. Once you have two braids, join the ends together in a mini twist or bun, then secure with pins.

5. Move on to the bottom section of hair and repeat steps 3 and 4.

6. Finish with a mist of hairspray to set. Pro tip: Add interest by trying a French braid in the middle and a Dutch on the bottom.

Try This

In a hurry? Skip the braiding and pull all sections straight back. Combine at the center of your head, then twist into bitty buns and secure with pins. Easy!

An elegant fishtail accent elevates the basic bun into weekend-worthy wear — perfect for all those occasions when you need to look fab in a flash.

Try This

Short on strands? Fake it with a faux braid headband wrapped around your top-knot. You can grab one at most drugstores or beauty supply stores.

1. Pull your hair into a high pony right on top of your head, then secure with an elastic.

2. Grab a 1" section of hair from the bottom of the pony, then fishtail it (see p. 122). Secure with a clear elastic, then use your fingers to gently loosen the braid from top to bottom—it'll make it thicker and flatter (check out p. 126).

3. To create lots of volume—and make your bun appear bigger— grab the remaining pony and gently tease the entire length, focusing on the base.

4. Wrap the tail around the pony base (just remember to keep your fishtailed piece separate), then pop in bobby pins all around to keep your new knot secure.

5. Gently tug on the bun to puff it out and shape it. Then grab the fishtailed piece and wrap it once around the bun. Secure with a bobby, then set everything with strong-hold hairspray.

fishtail bun

headband wrap

Who knew a simple elastic headband could create such a precious, polished style? Guaranteed to be your new go-to, just wrap and roll — it's really that easy.

1. This style works best with lots of texture. Start with unwashed locks, or quickly add large, messy curls to your mane with a 1½" iron.

2. Lightly tease the crown area, then spritz all over with a texturizing spray.

3. Use a comb to part strands to one side, then pull a few inches of hair forward.

4. Place the top of your elastic headband about an inch back from your forehead, then adjust it so the sides fit snugly right behind your ears and the bottom rests at the nape of your neck.

5. The elastic will create a "poof" at the back of your head. Smooth it out if needed, or slide the bottom part of band up a bit to create more body.

6. Leave a few tendrils hanging in the front, then pull the rest of front pieces back—above your ears and over the headband on both sides. Tuck into the elastic and wrap around once to hold hair in place. Adjust on both sides.

7. Scoop up remaining hair that's hanging down and pull it all into a wide, loose pony (but don't tie it off). Grab the bottom, then pull it all up and roll underneath the elastic.

8. Continue to tuck and pin strands as needed until you have all of your hair rolled underneath the headband. Mist with spray.

You can switch up the entire vibe of your 'do just by styling it with the right headband. Go glitzy for a Saturday-night movie...or try a femme, floral pattern for mini golf with your crew.

Loose curls and elegant twists are key to creating this ultra-sweet style. Lovely with a pony, but also perfect with low, messy braids and buns.

HAIR
DARE #6

SHARE YOUR SKILLS

Everyone has different styling strengths—so grab your girls and take turns swapping faves. You'll pick up plenty of new tricks, tips and techniques from each other...and maybe score some hair inspiration you never would have dreamed up solo.

1 Part hair on one side. Using a 1½" iron, curl all of your hair. (Check out the how-to on p. 58 for tips).

2 Pull front pieces forward on both sides, then separate the rest of your hair equally into three vertical sections: left side, middle and right side. Tie off each with clear elastics.

3 Separate the middle into two equal sections: top and bottom. Tie off the bottom section, and hold the top section in your hand.

4 Using a fine-toothed teasing tool, gently backcomb the roots of the entire section. Let it fall straight down over the pony you already created underneath.

5 Twist the left side of hair across to the right of the pony, then pin in place.

6 Twist the right side of hair across to the left of the pony, then pin in place.

7 Using a strong hair elastic, pull everything together into one pony. Grab a section of hair from the bottom of the pony, then wrap around the base to hide the tie. Slip in a bobby pin, then set everything with a quick mist of flexible hairspray.

twisted pony

pinned **perfection**

Barrettes, bobbies, clips—there are so many awesomely unexpected ways to wear these seemingly simple tress tools. Try the chevron-inspired style shown here, or get creative with your own designs.

1. Start with second-day hair, or prep your locks with a light mist of texturizing spray to help accessories stay snugly in place.

2. Pull hair into a side bun, topknot, low pony—whatever you want.

3. Pop in your accessories in a pretty pattern. Set with hairspray. That's it!

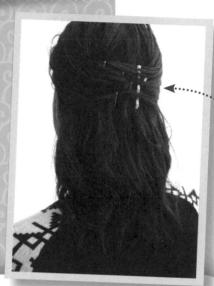

More things to do with bobby pins...

- Stack a few different shades in a cute color scheme.

- Cross a couple to make an "x" pattern.

- Tuck them vertically into your 'do (and use standout hues!).

- Stick a contrasting shade all over your updo, like black pins in platinum locks.

- Secure your half-up 'do by shaping pins into a triangular trio.

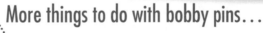

Tressipe

#DIY Hair Mask

WHAT YOU'LL NEED

- 1 banana
- 4 tbsp coconut oil (organic, unrefined)
- 8 ounces Greek yogurt (plain, full-fat)
- 2 tbsp olive oil

WHAT YOU'LL DO

1. Spoon coconut oil into a dish and microwave for 5 to 10 seconds, or until it becomes a creamy paste. Chop up the banana.

2. Combine all ingredients in a blender and mix until smooth. Pour into a bowl.

3. Apply to damp hair (use a spray bottle to spritz on some water if needed) from roots to tips. Work it through with your fingers and make sure to fully cover your ends. Tip: Massage your scalp—instant stress relief!

4. Pull hair up into a shower cap. After about 30 minutes, rinse thoroughly. Shampoo and condition as normal.

5. Enjoy your healthy, shiny hair!

HAIR Candy

Gilded Gemstone Barrette

Pick any stone you love and give it the glam treatment: a quick dip in a bit of gold! Pop this pretty right over a pony, or use it to pin back curls for a haute half-'do.

WHAT YOU'LL NEED

- Assorted gemstones (with at least one flat side)
- Basic metal hair barrette
- Gold craft paint
- Strong-hold craft glue

WHAT YOU'LL DO

1 Place the barrette on a flat surface. Below it, lay out your gems, making a pattern that'll fit the clip.

2 Working from left to right, take each gem and dip the bottoms in gold paint.

3 Lay gems on a paper plate, flat side down, keeping the stones in order. Let everything dry.

4 Cover the barrette with a layer of craft clue.

5 Place each gem on the barrette, then make any needed adjustments—like moving the stones up or down slightly to get the look you want.

6 Once everything is placed, lay the barrette's "good" side down on a paper towel. Let dry completely.

7 Rock it. (Pun intended!)

PARTY HAIR

Life's a celebration—so why not make each and every day as fun and glamorous as party night? Whether your schedule is stacked with chic soirées and dances or you just want to feel extra festive on a Friday, these snap-worthy styles will make you the belle of every bash. Shine on!

100
b-day girl bow

102
fresh twist

knotted **cord**

104

106

glitzed-out **volume**

108

retro **rings**

b-day girl **bow**

The basic bow gets a party-approved update when paired with a festive frock and placed atop beautifully bouncy curls.

1. Prep roots with a volumizing spray, then blow-dry and curl from roots to tips (see p. 58 for the how-to). To get bouncy ringlets, use a smaller wand (try a ½" or 1" barrel) and start wrapping from the root.

2. Grab a section of hair that's 3" to 4" wide near the "bang" area (the center of your forehead), then use a comb to gently tease the root area.

3. Secure with a clear elastic near the center of your head.

4. Push the elastic down and slightly forward, toward your face, creating volume in the front section.

5. Secure firmly with a bobby pin, then hide it by popping your bow right on top. Mist with medium-hold hairspray to set. Party perfect.

Try This

Want a completely custom bow to match your dream dress? Check out our DIY on p. 110—just skip the headband and attach to an alligator clip.

This classic coif gets a modern vibe thanks to tons of texture and a bit of messiness. Très chic, but surprisingly simple—just try our twisting trick.

HAIR
DARE #7

SPREAD THE LOVE

Whether it's your bestie's new bangs or your lab partner's ah-mazing updo at the dance, kick up the kindness and compliment other girls with great hair. You'll either make someone's day, or make a new friend. Win-win!

1 Start with second-day strands, or lightly mist clean hair with a combo of sea salt spray and dry texturizer. Then muss with fingers and tease roots all around.

2 Pull hair back into a ponytail near the nape of your neck (but don't tie it off).

3 Use your dominant hand to hold the base of the pony, then slide your other hand down to hold the ends of the tail.

4 Wrap the base around the pointer finger of your dominant hand once, then pull that finger up toward your crown as you twirl it. Your finger will be wrapped in hair at the center of your twist—that's okay.

5 While your dominant hand is holding the twist in place, use your other hand to pull up any hair that has fallen loose and spread it over the twist.

6 Tuck plenty of bobby pins into the bottom of the twist and along its crease to hold everything in place.

7 Pull down a few front pieces, then mist everything with hairspray for hold.

fresh twist

knotted cord

A few face-framing knots add oomph to any updo. Style with a sophisticated bun or pair with a pony to add fun flair.

1. Prep hair with texturizing spray and give roots a light tease.

2. Part hair to one side, then rub texturizing powder between your fingers (it'll give your strands some grip).

3. On the heavier side of your part, grab the two inches in front and split into 1" sections.

4. Cross them, then pull one side under the other to create a loose knot. Gently pull it tighter until you have a small ring near your part. Unless your hair is short, you'll still have the ends hanging out of the knot.

5. Tuck a bobby into the knot—it should be hidden, but will help keep everything in place.

6. Pick up the ends again and, like you're French braiding, add more hair to both sections.

7. Repeat the knotting process. Pin, then grab more hair and keep going.

8. Work your way to the nape of your neck, then pin and tie off. Pull hair into a pony and curl the ends, then wrap into a messy bun and pin.

Switch up the size of your knots—you could keep your cord teeny-tiny, or try bigger, looser loops. Better yet? Mix and match!

Want a festive finish for your cropped cut? Lots of volume and glitzy accent pieces are sure to get the party started.

+ TRESS S.O.S.

"It rained on my perfect party hair!"

Big nights out need a back-up plan—so always carry a kit containing these three style savers: a glam elastic headband, a hair tie and hairspray. If rain or humidity (or any other natural disaster) should cause your coif to go crazy, just throw hair into a messy topknot and slip on your sparkly band. Crisis averted!

1 Use a tail comb to part locks into three sections—everything between the ends of both your eyebrows is the middle. Next, brush down both sides.

2 Use a teasing tool to backcomb the middle section and create tons of bold body. Then gently brush through any kinks or craziness to give your poof a polished feel.

3 If you have super textured strands, rub cream oil between your hands and then slick along sides to hold hair down and get that fauxhawk feel. Have finer hair? A bit of hairspray or basic gel will do.

4 Pop a jeweled clip onto one side, above the ear. Time to dazzle!

glitzed-out volume

retro rings

1. Curl hair all over using a 2" iron for big, barrel waves.

2. Grab a 2" deep section of hair between the ends of both eyebrows. Clip into three equal parts.

3. Take one section, brush it out smooth, and then wrap around two fingers to create a pin curl.

4. Release, flatten it out and then wrap it until it's resting tightly against your head. Use a pin (or two) to keep it in place. Repeat on remaining sections.

5. Next, pull all your hair over one shoulder.

6. On the opposite side, grab the hair above your ear and begin twisting it. Add more as you go and work your way along your hairline toward the nape of your neck.

7. When you get to the other side, pop large hairpins in the twist to keep everything snug and secure. Mist with hairspray.

Try This

This look is lovely on chicas with short strands, too! Just curl hair with a smaller iron, then use plenty of pins to keep hair from slipping out of your rings.

Studded Metallic Bow

This edgy, embellished headband will up the glam factor on any style. We went monochrome and metallic, but you can also mix up your shades—try pretty pastels for spring or your class colors for a Spirit Week ensemble.

WHAT YOU'LL NEED

- Flat headband
- Rectangular piece of leather
- Thin strip of leather
- Thread
- Puff paint
- Craft clue

WHAT YOU'LL DO

1 Lay out your piece of leather with the good side facing up, then squeeze together at the center to create a bow shape.

2 Wrap plenty of thread around the middle area to hold the shape in place, then tie off in a snug knot and trim off any extra.

3 Position the bow on the side of the headband, then wrap your thin piece of leather around the threaded middle area.

4 Secure with glue, then wait for it to dry before cutting off any excess leather from the center of the bow.

5 Squeeze mini drops of puff paint all along the edges. When they dry, you'll have chic studs!

Tease, please!

Want to build body and get mega volume? Or prep your hair with tons of texture for a style that needs to stick? Here's how...

- Grab your two tools: texture spray and a teasing comb.
- Clip aside the top layer of your hair (or whatever falls on both sides of your part)—you never want to tease strands that are showing.
- Hold a section of hair straight up in the air and lightly mist the roots with texturizing spray.

- Starting an inch or so away from scalp (more inches = more body), run a teasing comb toward the roots a few times.
- Remember: Running any hair tool against the cuticle of your hair (aka in the direction of tip to root) is usually a no-no. But this technique (called back-combing) is totally fine in moderation—just be gentle and don't do it daily.
- Repeat on multiple sections to build volume in the areas where you need it. Or, if you're just prepping hair to get volume all over, select a handful of sections to tease all over your head.

BRAIDS

The secret to an amazing braid?
Practice. The five stunning styles
ahead are key to creating all the
braided looks in this book—and
once you've mastered them, the
pretty possibilities are endless. So
go ahead: Twist, cross, grab and
pull your way to perfect hair.

116

basic braid

118

fishtail braid

French braid

122

120

124

basic braid

It doesn't get any easier than this. If you're a total knotting newbie, start here and work your way up to trickier twists.

1. Start with three equal sections: left, right and middle.

2. Cross left over middle—now the original left section is in the middle.

3. Cross right over middle—now the original right section is in the middle.

4. Repeat and keep going!

5. And once you can't reach, pull hair over your shoulder, then finish and tie off.

This complete classic works well on every hair type. You'll follow the same format as the basic braid, but add in a bit more hair each time you cross.

1. Pull top section into three equal parts: left, right and middle.

2. Cross left over middle—now the original left section is the new middle section.

3. Cross right over middle—now the original right section is in the new middle section.

4. Repeat, returning to the left side to cross it over the middle again—but first, scoop up another section of hair from the left side of your head, then combine with the left section before crossing.

5. Repeat the same process on the right side, grabbing another section of hair and adding it to the right section before crossing to the middle.

6. Continue to repeat, picking up more hair each time you cross over.

7. When you reach the hairline, braid normally and tie off at the end.

French braid

Dutch braid

Once you've figured out the French, this twist is the cinchy next step. Also called an "inside-out" or "reverse French" braid, it uses the same technique—except you pull pieces under, not over, into the middle each time.

1. Pull top section into three equal parts: left, right and middle.

2. Cross left under middle—now the original left section is the new middle section.

3. Cross right under middle—now the original right section is in the new middle section.

4. Repeat, returning to the left side to cross it under the middle again—but first, scoop up another section of hair from the left side of your head, then combine with the left section before crossing underneath.

5. Repeat the same process on the right side, grabbing another section of hair and adding it to the right section before crossing under the middle.

6. Continue to repeat, picking up more hair each time you cross.

7. When you reach the hairline, continue to reverse braid normally (cross pieces under, not over) and tie off at the end.

The fancy fishtail braid is actually one of the easiest to catch onto (get it?). Move over, mermaids — you've got this.

1 Split hair into two equal parts.

2 Grab a small piece from the outside of the left part, and cross it over to join the right part.

3 Grab a small piece from the outside of the right part, and cross it over to join the left part.

4 Continue to repeat...

5 Work your way down, making sure to pull tightly each time. As you near the bottom, grab super small sections (or it might start looking like a regular braid.)

6 When you reach the bottom, tie with a clear elastic.

fishtail braid

cornrows

These mini microbraids share the same twisting technique with the Dutch braid—the difference is all in how you part and section these sweeties into a series of rows.

1 Section off your first row, then split it into three equal sections. Pin back the rest of your hair to keep it out of the way.

2 Cross right section under middle section (so it becomes the new middle section), then cross left section under middle section (so now it becomes the new middle section). Sound familiar? You're Dutch braiding! Get the full how-to on p.120.

3 Each time you cross from the right or left side, first pull in more hair to join that section. Remember to keep pulling tightly each move.

4 When you reach the end of your hair, pull tightly against the scalp and tie off with a tiny elastic band. Or, if you have longer hair, you can continue to reverse braid until you reach the ends.

5 Repeat in whatever pattern of rows you prefer.

Head over to p. 126 to see more cornrow technique tips.

STYLE HACKS

BRAID

Have lots of layers or short strands that stick out of your braid? Just curl hair first.

Rub texturizing powder between fingers before twisting—you'll get a great grip.

To keep a braid tight at the beginning of your twist, tie off with a clear elastic before you begin. Carefully snip it off with scissors when finished.

To get a bigger braid with tons of texture: Gently stretch apart with your fingers.

More fun with fishtails...

- Rock it super messy over one shoulder.
- Only braid halfway down the tail, then curl the rest.
- Sweep strands to the side, then braid a bold accent piece.
- Fishtail two front sections, then join at the back.

Consider when you cornrow...

- Always start with detangled, well-moisturized hair.

- Use the end of a tail comb to pull a perfect part when arranging your rows.

- Try twisting with both damp hair and with dry, stretched (if natural) hair—usually, every braider will pick a preference between the two.

- Remember to keep fingers close to the scalp as you braid—it'll help keep your cornrow tight.

- But don't twist too tightly to the point of pain—and if you ever notice red irritation or white bumps, remove the rows and treat yourself to a scalp massage.

Basic braid upgrades...

- Pop in a pretty accent piece to add unexpected interest.

- Style strands into pigtails. Keep it messy for a cool-girl vibe.

- Braid front sections, then join at the back for a halo effect.

- Braid two pigtails, then pull into a crown and pin in place.

PRODUCED BY KELSEY HAYWOOD
STYLED BY JESSICA D'ARGENIO WALLER
DESIGNED BY CHUN KIM
COVER PHOTOGRAPHED BY SEAN SCHEIDT

INTERIOR PHOTOGRAPHY
DEAN ALEXANDER • 7, 17, 21, 109, 113
BRION MCCARTHY • 10, 13, 31 (top), 40, 67
(bottom), 68 (right), 85-86, 93 (bottom), 126,
127 (top right)
SEAN SCHEIDT • 1, 15, 24-25, 27, 28-30, 31
(bottom), 32-34, 37-39, 41, 43,
46-49, 51-52, 55-57, 59, 64-66, 67 (top), 69-71,
72 (right), 73-74, 77, 81-84, 87-89, 91-92, 93
(top), 95, 97-101, 103-105, 107-108, 110-111,
114-125, 127 (all but top right), 128

HAIR & MAKEUP
LEAH SARAH BASSETT, LUIS BUJIA,
ROXANNE FARIAS-WALSH,
STACY LEIGH, ANDREA MITCHELL

INTERNS
CHEYENNE DERMODY,
LAURISE MCMILLIAN,
BECKY WHELAN

CLOTHING & ACCESSORIES
AMERICAN APPAREL,
ARIZONA, BAN.DO, CAMEO,
COTTON CANDY, DOLORIS
PETUNIA, ELLE, EVERLY,
EMI JAY, GLAMOROUS,
J.O.A., KITSCH, KLING,
L.L. BEAN, LEVIS, LINE & DOT,
LOVEMARKS, LUSH, LULU*S,
LULUS.COM, MIA BEAUTY,
M.J. DESIGNER PARIS,
MORNING APPLE,
MUSTARD SEED, NAKAMOL,
NFL JUNIORS, O'NEILL,
PURE HYPE, RHYTHM, UNDER ARMOUR,
URBAN HALO, URBANOG,
THE VINTAGE SHOP, ZOE LTD